SURVIVAL
HANDBOOK
POLAR

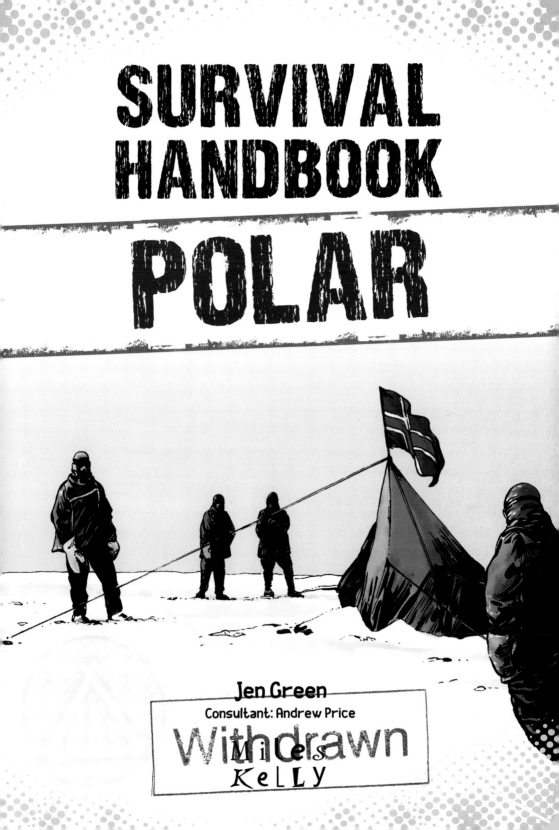

SURVIVAL
HANDBOOK
POLAR

Jen Green

Consultant: Andrew Price

Miles
Kelly

First published in 2012 by Miles Kelly Publishing Ltd
Harding's Barn, Bardfield End Green,
Thaxted, Essex, CM6 3PX, UK

Copyright © Miles Kelly Publishing Ltd 2012

This edition published 2014

2 4 6 8 10 9 7 5 3 1

Publishing Director Belinda Gallagher
Creative Director Jo Cowan
Editorial Director Rosie Neave
Design Manager Simon Lee
Image Manager Liberty Newton
Production Manager Elizabeth Collins
Reprographics Stephan Davis,
Jennifer Hunt, Thom Allaway

ISBN 978-1-78209-435-7

Printed in China

British Library Cataloguing-in-Publication Data
A catalogue record for this book is available from the British Library

Important notice
This book provides useful information for hypothetical
situations in which individuals may find themselves. Some
of the techniques described in this book should only be
used in dire emergencies, when the survival of individuals
depends upon them. The publisher and author cannot be
held responsible for any injuries, damage, loss, or
prosecutions resulting from the use or misuse of any
of the information in this book.

Made with paper from a sustainable forest

www.mileskelly.net
info@mileskelly.net

CONTENTS

IMAGINE YOU ARE STRANDED IN THE POLAR WILDERNESS.

How would you cope?

This book explores what it would be like to be in a survival situation, and tells you what to expect. Look out for the 'Try this at home' panels for tips and activities that you can practise safely in the comfort of your own home.

WARNING!

Never put yourself in danger and always ask the permission of a responsible adult before trying any of the activities in this book.

GET INFORMED

Environment

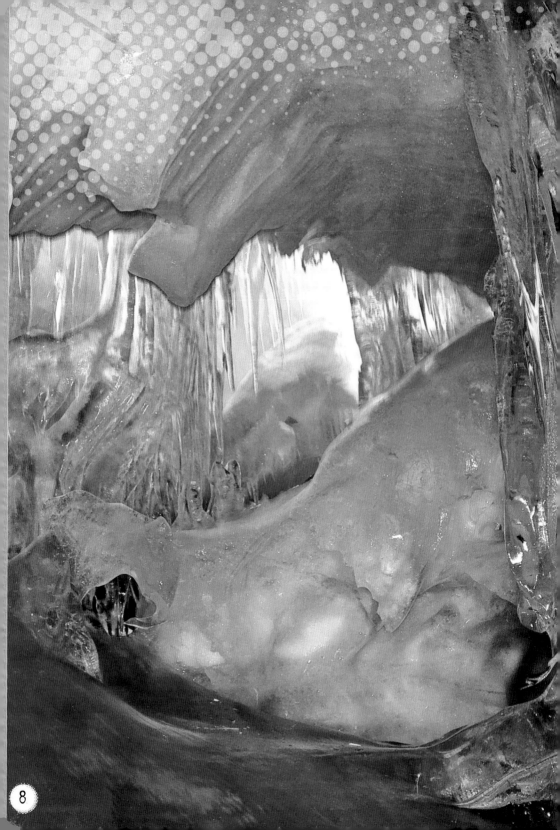

Ends of the Earth

THE POLAR REGIONS are the ultimate survival challenge. Snow and ice stretch to the horizon. In the intense cold, exposed skin begins to freeze in seconds. Navigation is extremely tricky. Food is scarce, and most of it has to be killed before you eat it. **Could you cope in this amazingly hostile place?**

North Pole

Sun's rays strike the polar regions at an oblique (shallow) angle

Sun's rays

Equator

Sun's rays

Sun's rays hit the Equator at a direct angle, making this the hottest part of Earth's surface

Sun's rays

South Pole

Polar zones

The polar regions lie in the far north and south of the planet. They are bounded by the Arctic and Antarctic Circles. As a round, rocky ball, Earth's surface curves away towards the Poles. The curve means that the Sun's rays are always weak in the polar regions – that's why it's always cold.

← The curvature of the Earth makes the Sun's rays weak. They also have further to travel through the atmosphere to reach the Poles.

Extreme seasons

Polar regions experience the most extreme seasons on Earth. This is because Earth tilts as it moves around the Sun. In summer, each Pole tilts towards the Sun, and is bathed in sunlight 24 hours a day. In winter each Pole tilts away from the Sun. The 24-hour darkness and bitter cold test your physical and mental endurance to the limit.

↑ The perpetual daylight of the polar summer makes it hard to sleep, and it's easy to get exhausted.

Arctic wilderness

THE ARCTIC IS A REMOTE, icy realm with little dry land. The dazzling whiteness stretching on all sides is sea ice, covering a dark, freezing-cold ocean. In this shifting world, where sea currents jostle floating ice, **nothing is quite what it seems**.

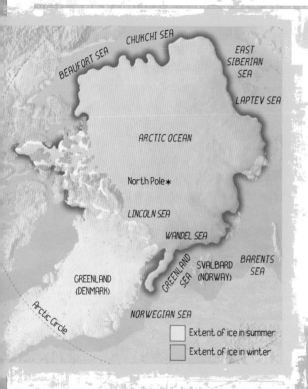

CHUKCHI SEA
EAST SIBERIAN SEA
BEAUFORT SEA
LAPTEV SEA
ARCTIC OCEAN
North Pole ✴
LINCOLN SEA
WANDEL SEA
GREENLAND SEA
SVALBARD (NORWAY)
BARENTS SEA
GREENLAND (DENMARK)
NORWEGIAN SEA
Arctic Circle

Extent of ice in summer
Extent of ice in winter

The far North

The Arctic Ocean covers most of the area within the Arctic Circle. This huge icy ocean is bounded by the northernmost parts of North America, Scandinavia, and Siberia in Russia. Greenland is the largest landmass in the Arctic. The world's largest island, it is almost entirely covered by an ice cap up to 3 km thick.

← Ice covering the Arctic Ocean expands in winter and contracts in summer.

⬇ Plants bloom during the brief Arctic summer when the snow melts.

The tundra

The High Arctic (the region closest to the North Pole) is always covered by ice and snow. Further south lie treeless lowlands – the tundra. In winter, this too is snow-covered, but in summer it becomes a marshland. Caribou (reindeer) and many birds migrate there in spring to raise their young, so food is plentiful in summer. But come the autumn, most animals follow the warm weather south.

Arctic peoples

The Arctic has been inhabited for thousands of years, despite the harsh conditions. The Inuit of North America traditionally hunt animals to live. Their survival skills are honed by bitter experience, and passed down through generations. To survive in the polar regions you will need to learn those skills from a local guide.

⬆ The Nenets of Russia live along the Arctic Ocean, and herd reindeer for transport and food.

North Pole

The North Pole is the most northerly place on Earth, where 1.8-m-thick sea ice covers a restless ocean. The first expedition to reach the Pole was probably led by US navy officer Robert Peary, in 1909. The first outsiders to explore the Arctic were the Vikings, who reached the shores of Greenland in 982 AD.

⬆ American explorer Robert Peary claimed to be first to reach the North Pole, but some experts have disputed this.

Be on your guard

A variety of animals live on the Arctic ice and in the surrounding waters, and walruses are among the most dangerous. Both males and females have long, pointed tusks that can be used as lethal weapons. It's best to steer well clear, particularly if there are young in the group.

➡ A male walrus can measure 6 m in length and weigh up to 1.7 tonnes.

THE ANTARCTIC is even more hostile than the Arctic. A vast, icy continent twice the size of Australia occupies virtually the whole region. Surrounded by huge floating ice shelves and the stormiest sea on Earth, **Antarctica is a daunting, terrifying place**.

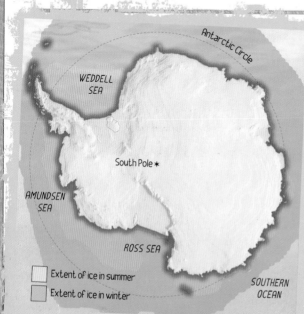

Antarctic Circle

WEDDELL
SEA

South Pole *

AMUNDSEN
SEA

ROSS SEA

SOUTHERN
OCEAN

☐ Extent of ice in summer
☐ Extent of ice in winter

Earth's highest content

The vast landmass of Antarctica is covered by an ice cap up to 4 km thick. Jagged peaks stick up out of the ice. The mountainous terrain combined with the dome of the ice sheet make this Earth's highest continent. High on the windswept plateau, temperatures are even colder than at sea level.

← Antarctica is Earth's fifth-largest continent. Huge floating ice shelves occupy large bays.

Survival foods

Almost no plants grow in Antarctica. The climate inland is too harsh for animals to survive, so there is no food there. Sea temperatures are actually milder than on land, and marine life such as seals, fish and penguins is abundant. If short of food in Antarctica, your only option is to head for the coast.

↑ Penguins provided food for past Antarctic expeditions, but they are now protected.

Who lives there?

Antarctica has never been inhabited by humans. In the 1820s the rocky shores were discovered by seal hunters. Following exploration in the early 1900s, many countries laid claim to land in Antarctica, but in 1959 a treaty declared the continent could only be used for science. Today, it is inhabited exclusively by scientists, living on about 80 research bases. All of them undergo rigorous survival training.

← Scientists study ice caves that have formed in a volcanic part of Antarctica, where hot rocks underground warm the surface.

South Pole

The most southerly point on Earth lies far inland. The US research base here is built on ice 3 km thick. The only way to reach the base is by air, but flights are regularly cancelled because of hurricane-force winds. The average temperature at the South Pole is −49°C.

↓ McMurdo Station, also called Mac Town, lies on the edge of the vast Ross Ice Shelf, not far from an active volcano, Mount Erebus.

WOW!

The largest settlement in Antarctica is the US base at McMurdo. More than 1100 people live there in summer, but only 250 stay for winter.

Life in the freezer

DAILY CONDITIONS in the polar regions are like living in a freezer. Cold is the main obstacle to survival, and exposure and frostbite (see pages 40-41) are constant threats. On the coldest days in the Arctic or Antarctic, **water tossed into the air will freeze before it hits the ground.**

➡ A mountaineer digs out his tent during a blizzard on Mount Vaughan in Antarctica. Snow is a good insulator, but a heavy fall can wreck your tent.

Extreme cold

Winter conditions last for nine months of the year in the polar regions. In the Arctic, temperatures may rise to 10°C in summer, but fall to −40°C in winter. Antarctica is even colder. The coldest outdoor temperature ever recorded (−89°C) occurred here in 1983.

WIND CHILL

Howling winds make icy temperatures feel colder. This is called wind chill. The chart below shows how wind chill affects temperature. For example, a 30 km/h wind makes a temperature of −5°C feel like −13°C.

	Temperature (°C)												
Wind speed (km/h)	0	−5	−10	−15	−20	−25	−30	−35	−40	−45	−50	−55	−60
6	−2	−8	−14	−19	−25	−31	−37	−42	−48	−54	−60	−65	−71
10	−3	−9	−15	−21	−27	−33	−39	−45	−51	−57	−63	−69	−75
15	−4	−11	−17	−23	−29	−35	−41	−48	−54	−60	−66	−72	−78
20	−5	−12	−18	−24	−30	−37	−43	−49	−56	−62	−68	−76	−81
25	−6	−12	−19	−25	−32	−38	−44	−51	−57	−64	−70	−77	−83
30	−6	−13	−20	−26	−33	−39	−46	−52	−59	−65	−72	−78	−85
35	−7	−14	−20	−27	−33	−40	−47	−53	−60	−66	−73	−80	−86
40	−7	−14	−21	−27	−34	−41	−48	−54	−61	−68	−74	−81	−88
45	−8	−15	−21	−28	−35	−42	−48	−55	−62	−69	−75	−82	−89
50	−8	−15	−22	−29	−35	−42	−49	−56	−63	−69	−76	−83	−90

WOW!

Antarctica is the windiest place on Earth – wind speeds of over 320 km/h have been recorded. In the early 1900s, Australian explorer Douglas Mawson wrote of Antarctica: "We have found the kingdom of blizzards. We have come to an accursed land."

↓ Whiteout conditions are extremely perilous. You can become disorientated just a few steps from shelter.

Blizzards and whiteouts

A blizzard strikes when strong winds accompany heavy snowfall. Whirling snow crystals fill the air, reducing visibility to zero. This is called a whiteout. Severe storms have been known to keep explorers in their tents for days. Prepare for a whiteout by fixing ropes or flags along essential routes, such as between the camp and toilet area.

SURVIVE A BLIZZARD

1. Remain in your shelter and sit out the storm. Be patient. Only go outside if necessary.
2. If camping in heavy snowfall, you may need to clear snow from the tent periodically, or the weight could make it collapse.
3. Beware deep drifts of blown snow in hollows.
4. Tightly fasten clothing before leaving shelter. Howling winds will drive snow into small gaps around the neck, zips and cuffs.

Polar deserts

The polar regions are technically deserts because so little rain falls there. The Arctic receives less than 25 cm of rain annually. The Antarctic gets even less – it's drier than the driest desert. Little rain falls in the polar regions because all moisture is locked up as ice.

↑ Lack of cloud cover means that glare from snow and ice is a serious risk during the polar summer, leading to headaches and snowblindness (see page 83).

Treacherous terrain

DEEP SNOW AND ICE make for a perilous environment. On land, glaciers may be cut by crevasses (deep open cracks). Avalanches are a danger in hilly country. Icebergs and floating ice are a menace in polar waters. In summer, solid ice turns slushy, and thin ice can give way, plunging you into icy water. **Death through exposure could quickly follow.**

⬆ During the British Antarctic expedition of 1910–12, one team member had to be hauled out using sledge-rope after plunging into a crevasse.

Rivers of ice

Glaciers form as layers of snow packed down to form ice. The weight of the ice sets the glacier sliding downhill until it reaches the coast, where chunks of ice 'calve' (break off to form icebergs). Crevasses are deep cracks in glaciers. They are particularly dangerous after snowfall, when a thin bridge of snow may hide a yawning gap. Tall columns of ice called seracs are another hazard, as these can topple without warning.

Icebergs

These floating chunks of ice are a danger to shipping. Seven-eighths of an iceberg's bulk lies hidden below the water's surface, so you need to give them plenty of space to avoid collision. Steer even further away in a small boat or canoe – icebergs can suddenly flip over without warning, creating a wave that could swamp your boat.

⬇ In the Southern Ocean, icebergs are mostly flat-topped, having broken off the ice cliffs that edge the coast.

Beware bogs

In summer, snow melts on the Arctic tundra. The meltwater cannot drain away through the permanently frozen ground, so it pools at the surface. It can be very difficult to make your way through the maze of bogs, pools and streams, whether travelling by canoe or wading on foot.

SURVIVE AN AVALANCHE

1. You can't outrun an avalanche, but you may be able to run to the side of one.
2. If the snow starts to pull you under, use a swimming motion to remain near the surface.
3. As the avalanche stops, cup your hands to make an air space in front of your face, and then try to kick and claw your way to the surface.
4. Push your arm upwards for the best chance of being spotted.

⬆ In summer, the countless streams that criss-cross the tundra make progress painfully slow.

⬅ Warmer temperatures during the summer melt the ice covering lakes, rivers and the ocean, making the going hazardous.

Sea ice

In autumn, polar seas freeze and form drifting ice floes. When the ice floes thicken they become pack ice, which can crush ships but at least forms a solid surface for travel by skis, sledge or snowmobile. In summer, sea ice breaks up, forming gaps called leads. Thin ice makes the going treacherous. For more advice on crossing ice, see pages 72-73.

Polar predators

THE ARCTIC IS SURPRISINGLY RICH IN WILDLIFE. Only animals that do not rely on vegetation can survive in the High Arctic. Unfortunately, that includes some of the very **few species on Earth that view humans as prey.**

BEWARE BEARS

In the lands south of the Arctic, people traditionally call bears 'masters of the forest'. These huge, powerful mammals are among the largest land animals and they have few natural enemies – except humans.

Polar bear

The polar bear is the ultimate Arctic predator. Its main weapons are its canine teeth and huge clawed paws that can strike with the force of a sledgehammer. The bear's ultra-keen sense of smell can detect prey up to 30 km away – and that includes humans. In the Arctic you need to carry a rifle to defend yourself against these ferocious bears.

Grizzly bear

Grizzly bears are a hazard on the tundra. Rearing up to 3 m in height on their back legs, these massive animals are surprisingly fast runners. They can be aggressive, and females with cubs are particularly dangerous. If a grizzly approaches, try to keep calm. Back away slowly facing the bear. If attacked, play dead or fight back.

Call of the wild

Wolves are top predators of the Arctic. Armed with strength and cunning, the pack works as a team to bring down prey as large as caribou. However, wolves rarely attack humans. At night you may hear their eerie howling, but your campfire should keep them at bay.

TIP

Mosquitoes are pests on the tundra. Wear a mosquito net over your head, and make sure your cuffs are fastened and your trousers are tucked into your boots.

TRY THIS AT HOME   **IDENTIFYING TRACKS**

Arctic peoples can identify animals such as bears and wolves from their tracks. They can even tell how many animals are in the group, and how fast they are moving. Look in books or on the Internet for help recognizing tracks, and then practise identifying wildlife from prints you find in mud or snow. For more on tracking, see pages 58–59.

Polar bear

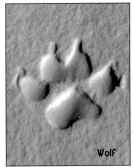
Wolf

⬆ Animal tracks show up most clearly in snow, but also in the mud along the banks of rivers, lakes and streams.

MARINE PREDATORS

Danger lurks in polar seas as well as on land. Both Arctic and Antarctic waters are home to orcas – the top killers of the oceans. Even far from land in the Arctic, you aren't safe from dreaded polar bears.

Leopard seal

Killer whale

The leopard seal is one of the most feared creatures in Antarctica. Weighing up to 380 kg, it is a fast and powerful killer, armed with needle-sharp teeth. It mainly preys on penguins, and will ram floating ice where penguins are resting to tip them into the water.

Orcas or killer whales roam the Arctic and Southern oceans. These brainy mammals work as a team to target seals and even large whales. They have been known to menace small boats, but you should be fairly safe unless you fall into the water.

TIP

Polar bears are known to chase canoers. Fire a warning shot in the air to scare the bear away. If it carries on coming, you may have to shoot to kill.

Elephant seal

Bull elephant seals are a menace on Antarctic coasts in the breeding season. The 4-tonne males come ashore to battle for the females, lunging at each other with canine teeth. Most of their fury is directed at each other, but you need to keep well clear.

NOTES

GET READY

THE POLAR REGIONS exert a strong pull over many people. Explorers are lured by the promise of fame or adventure. Survival experts go to test their skills, or experience the wild beauty of these untouched places. Whatever your reasons, **thorough preparation will be vital to the success of your trip**.

Preparation

A polar expedition involves months of preparation. You need to gather the right equipment and get fit through rigorous training. You should research the area, and above all, practise skills such as fire-lighting until they become second nature. Only then will you have a chance of surviving if emergency strikes, and you are stranded without shelter.

⬇ The ability to start a fire quickly and easily is an essential survival skill.

TIP

Research accounts of previous expeditions in the area you intend to visit. These will provide vital advice for your own trip.

⬅ Traditionally most Inuit food came from the sea. These hunters are after seals.

Learning the ropes

Arctic peoples are expert at cold-weather survival. For centuries, this seemingly hostile environment has met all their needs for food, water, clothing and shelter. To survive here you must learn to dress, hunt, eat, sleep and think like an Arctic inhabitant!

Choosing your kit

CHOOSE YOUR KIT CAREFULLY. You will need a strong tent, warm sleeping bag and a mat for camping. You should include tools such as a snow shovel, and a signalling kit in case you get into difficulties. Travel games will come in handy **if bad weather keeps you in your tent**!

Polar gear

Don't skimp on quality when it comes to essentials for a polar trip. Your gear needs to be tough to withstand the harshest conditions on Earth!

Laser flare

Mirror

Flashlight

Whistle

Mobile phone

Maps

GPS (global positioning system)

Multi-tool

Matches

Compass

Ice axe

Candles

Snow shovel

Lighter

Tarpaulin

Fire steel

Mini survival kit

Bivvy bag

➡ Carry a mini survival kit on all expeditions. Include a nightlight, matches, a small torch, a penknife, fishing line and hooks, a small mirror, a whistle, a mini sewing kit, superglue, wire and string. Seal it with plastic tape.

Travel gear

You'll need ski poles and skis or snowshoes to move over snowy terrain. An ice axe and crampons are useful to scale icy slopes. If you intend to cross water you'll need a canoe. For more on travel turn to pages 67-74.

← Heavy gear should be loaded onto a sledge that slides easily over the ice.

TIP

Practise using equipment such as a GPS while wearing thick gloves. Read instructions on new equipment carefully to make sure you know how it works.

WOW!

Traditionally, Arctic peoples loaded their gear onto sledges pulled by huskies, or (in Siberia) sleighs pulled by caribou. Today snowmobiles are more often used than animals.

KEY

1 First aid kit
2 Torch
3 Waterproof and warm clothing
4 Water bottle
5 Cooking equipment
6 Change of clothes
7 Matches
8 Compass
9 Snacks
10 Sleeping bag and mat
11 Tent

↑ A rucksack with several pockets and compartments stores essential items and allows you to reach them quickly.

TRY THIS AT HOME — A PRACTICE HIKE

Pack your rucksack and take it on a practice hike, in snowy or hilly terrain if possible. A long, gruelling walk will help you work out the weight you can comfortably carry. Carrying a heavy pack will help you concentrate on what you can leave out! Make sure you ask an adult to accompany you.

Packing

Pack your gear in a heavy-duty rucksack. Items that you will need last or least should be near the bottom. Pack essential items in pockets or at the top. Put clothes and other kit in plastic bags to sort and waterproof your gear.

WEARING THE RIGHT GEAR can make the difference between life and death in the polar regions. You need to cover every inch of your body to guard against frostbite. Wearing lots of layers is **the key to keeping warm**.

Polar outfit

Several layers of light clothing will keep you warm and dry in subzero temperatures.

Outer layer protects you from the elements. Your hooded jacket and overtrousers should be wind- and water-proof but breathable, to allow sweat to escape.

Layer 3

Layer 1

Undergarmets fit snugly at neck and cuffs

Second layer provides warmth

High neck zips up

A fleecy hat or balaclava is a must to maintain warmth

Layer 2

Inner gloves keep your hands warm under your outer mittens

Layer 4

Thin underclothes such as a thermal top and long-johns keep you warm and wick away sweat.

Add a second pair of socks, thicker than the first

Loose-fitting, breathable garments such as a cotton shirt and trousers provide insulation.

A fleece, wool sweater or fibre-pile suit add warmth.

Unsuitable suits

Early polar explorers wore tweed suits and woolly jumpers! Non-breathable clothing trapped sweat, which froze in extreme cold. A British explorer described the result: "Our clothing was as hard as boards and stuck out from our bodies in every imaginable angle."

← Members of Scott's Antarctic team of 1910-12 wore fabrics designed for the British climate that did not perform well in polar conditions.

INSULATION

Wearing four or five thin layers is better than two thick ones. Air trapped between each layer provides insulation. You can also put on and shed layers to adjust your body temperature as you work, travel or rest.

Protective layer (orange) keeps out wind and wet

Body heat is trapped by the insulation layer (light blue)

Inner layer (dark blue) wicks moisture away from skin

C.O.L.D.

The letters C.O.L.D. spell the key to polar survival.

C Keep your whole body COVERED and CLEAN – dirt and grime reduce insulation.

O Avoid OVERHEATING. Sweat makes your clothing damp, which chills your body.

L LOOSE-FITTING LAYERS trap warm air and allow you to move freely.

D Keep DRY at all costs. Wet clothing loses its ability to insulate.

Layers of fur

Traditional Arctic dress consists of two layers of animal skins: warm, thin undergarments with fur facing inwards, and tough outer clothes with fur facing outwards. Hides are softened by chewing, and sewn with bone needles and reindeer-sinew thread.

➡ The skins of polar animals repel moisture and provide warmth.

Food and medicine

A BALANCED DIET with a variety of foods is essential for staying healthy on a polar expedition. You should pack a first aid kit and know how to use it. **Go on a first aid course before your trip.**

FOOD PYRAMID

A food pyramid shows the proportion of each type of food that is needed for a balanced diet.

Chocolate
Sweets

Small amounts of fatty and sugary foods provide energy and are good for morale.

Nuts
Cheese

Meat, fish, dairy products, nuts, eggs and beans provide protein. You may be able to obtain meat and fish from the wild.

Berries
Dried fruit

Fruit and vegetables provide vitamins, minerals and fibre. Berries grow on the tundra in autumn but at other times you'll need to carry dried fruit.

Rice

Carbohydrates in pasta, rice, bread, potatoes and crackers provide energy. Dried versions last well.

Pasta   Crackers

Cooking kit

Hot food and drinks are essential on polar expeditions. Practise making a few simple and nourishing meals before you go.

Cutlery
Tin opener
Stove
Saucepan
Mess tin
Tin mug

Arctic diet

Meat is the staple of the traditional Arctic diet – mostly seal, but also hare, bird, whale, fish and polar bear. In summer, eggs and berries provide variety. This diet was thought to be lacking in vitamins, but we now know that foods such as whale skin contain vitamin C.

➡ A young herdsman from Arctic Russia chews on a piece of caribou flesh. Meat provides vital energy to maintain body warmth.

Keep it varied

Eating the same thing every day lowers morale, so you need to take a range of foods that fulfil your dietary needs and keep you energized. Polar explorers of the early 1900s mainly lived on pemmican – a paste of pounded meat and fat. It was high in protein but practically indigestible, and very boring.

⬆ Pemmican is convenient to carry, but makes for a very boring diet.

WOW!

In 1845, British naval officer Sir John Franklin led an expedition through Arctic waters, taking a store of beef in cans sealed with lead. Eating it gave the men lead poisoning, and in their weakened state the entire crew perished of cold and starvation.

EXPEDITION FOODS AND TRAIL SNACKS

1. Dried, tinned and powdered foods keep better than fresh produce.

2. Snacks such as cereal bars, crisps and chocolate provide energy on the move.

3. Moist foods will freeze in polar conditions. This can help to preserve some foods, but precious fuel will be needed to defrost as well as cook it.

4. Don't forget salt, to replace salt you lose as you sweat.

First aid kit

A first aid kit is vital to treat injuries. Don't forget painkillers, lip salve and suncream. Pack a mosquito net and insect repellent for a trip to the tundra.

➡ First aid gear should be sealed in a watertight box or bag, and stowed where you can reach it quickly at all times.

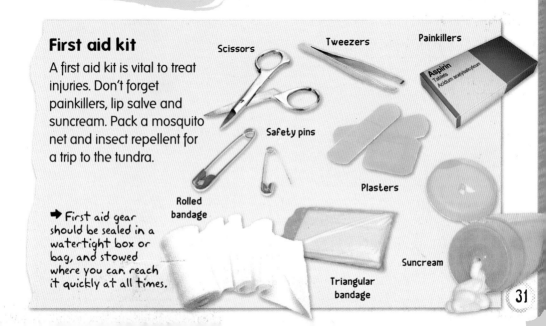

Scissors

Tweezers

Painkillers

Aspirin
Tablets
Acidum acetylsalicylicum

Safety pins

Plasters

Rolled bandage

Triangular bandage

Suncream

Before you go

GET READY FOR YOUR TRIP by training in environments that mimic polar conditions as closely as possible. Build fitness through exercise such as swimming or jogging. You need to prepare mentally as well as physically by researching and **practising survival skills**.

Research

Discover as much as you can about the way of life in the area you intend to visit. Read up on polar survival and the feats of explorers. Learn a few words of the local language. You already know some Inuit words, such as anorak and kayak!

← The hut used by Scott's Antarctic expedition of 1910–12 is still intact, with its stores.

Planning

Plan each stage of the expedition thoroughly. Make back-up plans to cover potential problems such as bad weather, delay or injury. Leave written details of your trip with a friend, and instruct them to raise the alarm if you don't appear at the appointed place and time.

WOW!

Some explorers have hardened their bodies for a polar trip by taking ice-cold baths!

TRY THIS AT HOME — **DEVELOP MAP-READING SKILLS**

Knowing how to read a map is a must on an expedition. Study a local map. Check the symbols shown against the key. Make sure you understand how features such as ice, bridges, cliffs and scree are shown.

KEY

Coniferous forest	
Body of water	
Bog	
Cliff	
Scree	
Hiking path	

TRUE STORY

RACE TO THE SOUTH POLE
Robert Falcon Scott

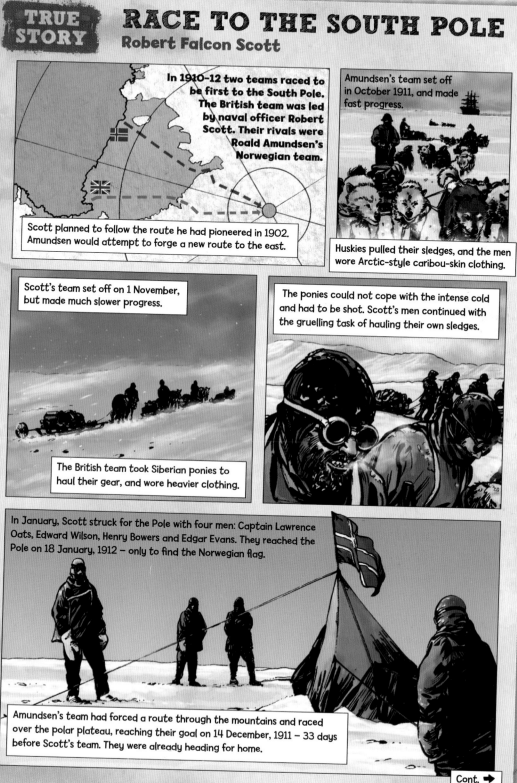

In 1910–12 two teams raced to be first to the South Pole. The British team was led by naval officer Robert Scott. Their rivals were Roald Amundsen's Norwegian team.

Scott planned to follow the route he had pioneered in 1902. Amundsen would attempt to forge a new route to the east.

Amundsen's team set off in October 1911, and made fast progress.

Huskies pulled their sledges, and the men wore Arctic-style caribou-skin clothing.

Scott's team set off on 1 November, but made much slower progress.

The British team took Siberian ponies to haul their gear, and wore heavier clothing.

The ponies could not cope with the intense cold and had to be shot. Scott's men continued with the gruelling task of hauling their own sledges.

In January, Scott struck for the Pole with four men: Captain Lawrence Oates, Edward Wilson, Henry Bowers and Edgar Evans. They reached the Pole on 18 January, 1912 – only to find the Norwegian flag.

Amundsen's team had forced a route through the mountains and raced over the polar plateau, reaching their goal on 14 December, 1911 – 33 days before Scott's team. They were already heading for home.

Cont. ➡

Scott wrote in his diary:

The POLE. Yes, but under very different circumstances from those expected. Great God! This is an awful place and terrible enough for us to have laboured to it without the reward of priority.

Scott and his men started on the return journey. By now they were all suffering from a combination of starvation, cold and scurvy.

On 17 February Evans slipped into a coma and died.

On 17 March they lost a second man – Captain Oates had been suffering from severe frostbite. Knowing he was slowing his companions down, he made the decision to walk out of the tent and freeze to death in the bitter cold.

Scott wrote in his diary: "We knew that Oates was walking to his death... it was the act of a brave man and an English gentleman."

The remaining three men perished from cold and starvation in their tent only a few days later.

Scott and two others died 18 km south of One Ton Depot.

The race to the South Pole was over. Amundsen's team completed their journey successfully through careful planning and their use of Arctic survival techniques.

NOTES

GET SAFE

Basic survival skills

First things first

THE POLAR REGIONS are a battleground for survival. Minute by minute, you face the challenge of keeping warm and guarding against frostbite. As soon as you stop moving, you need to find shelter and light a fire to melt drinking water. These four basics – warmth, fire, shelter and water – are top priorities **both in an emergency and on a planned expedition**.

Organize your group

In a group, you need to be organized to work together efficiently. You could match tasks to people's skills, but make sure everyone does their fair share of chores such as collecting fuel and melting snow.

↓ Members of a large polar expedition organize their gear before beginning their trek.

Build a snow hole

A snow hole provides emergency shelter. Find a snow bank with at least 2.5 m of snow. Use a shovel to dig a tunnel that slopes downwards at first, then upwards. Hollow out a sleeping platform at the end. Loosely close the entrance with a snow-block or a large piece of kit, such as your rucksack. Use a stick to make a ventilation hole.

Smooth the inside walls to discourage drips

Make an air hole with a ski pole or stick

Sleeping platform raised above 'sink' of cold air

Cold air gets trapped here

39

Fighting the cold

COLD IS THE MAIN ENEMY in the Arctic and Antarctic. Temperatures of –30°C bring high risk of frostbite and hypothermia – that's when your body temperature **dips dangerously low**.

Frostbite

Frostbite occurs when skin and flesh freezes. Extreme cases can lead to gangrene (death of tissue) and risk of amputation. Tight clothing increases the risk of frostbite by restricting blood flow to hands and feet, so make sure clothing is loose.

⬇ In cases of severe frostbite, amputating (cutting off) the worst-affected areas is a last resort.

STAGES OF FROSTBITE

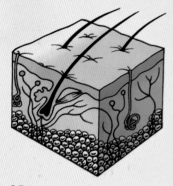

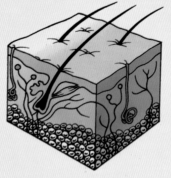

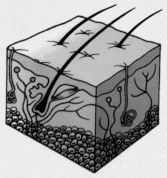

1 Frostnip
Skin looks pale and waxy, and feels painful and itchy. Only upper skin is affected and damage is not permanent.

2 Superficial frostbite
Skin becomes white, hard and numb. Blisters develop. Deep tissues are not affected, most injuries heal quite quickly.

3 Deep frostbite
Tissue below the skin freezes. Skin turns blue, then black, and blisters. Surgery may be needed and damage takes months to heal.

Hypothermia

Hypothermia usually strikes when you are cold, wet and tired. You lose more heat than your body can generate and your temperature drops below 35°C. The best way to avoid hypothermia is to wear warm, dry clothing, eat hot food, drink plenty of water, and stay active. See pages 82–83 for more information.

⬇ Hot food or drink will provide instant warmth for anyone suspected of suffering from hypothermia.

AVOIDING FROSTBITE AND HYPOTHERMIA

1. Wear a windproof layer over several layers of warm clothing. If you feel cold, put on another layer.
2. Keep every part of the body covered. Don't remove gloves to do fiddly jobs.
3. Make every effort to keep dry. Beat snow off clothes before you approach the fire or enter your tent.
4. In a group, pair up and check one another for signs of frostbite.

WOW!

In 1999, a man building a cabin in subzero temperatures in northern Canada put nails in his mouth to hold them. The metal nails stuck to his lips, taking a chunk of flesh with them when prized off.

HEAT CONDUCTION

Different materials conduct (carry) heat away from the body at different speeds. For example, aluminium conducts heat 2000 times faster than wood, which is why your hands get cold much faster if you're holding a shovel with a metal handle than if you're holding one with a wooden handle. Ice conducts heat 86 times faster than air, so it's vital not to sit or lie down on snow or ice. Instead, cover the ground with an insulating layer such as spruce branches or canvas.

Materials	
1	Aluminium
2	Steel
3	Ice
4	Water
5	Wood
6	Air

⬅ This table shows some common materials, ordered by thermal conductivity.

TIP

Extremities such as nose, ears, fingers and toes are prone to frostbite. Wiggle your toes and fingers to improve circulation, and wear several pairs of socks and mittens.

Emergency shelter

IF YOU FIND YOURSELF IN THE OPEN without a tent, you will need to improvise shelter. Luckily, snow is an excellent building material, and provides insulation. Building a shelter is hard work, which will **help you to keep warm**!

WOW!

Air spaces between snow crystals makes snow an excellent insulator. The temperature inside your shelter won't drop below -10°C, even if it's extremely cold outside.

BUILD A SNOW TRENCH

A snow trench is a simple temporary shelter. Use a shovel, saw or knife to cut snow blocks.

1 Mark out an area long and wide enough to take a camping mat with 0.5 m to spare at each end. Excavating snow in blocks, dig a trench to a depth of 0.5 m.

Ideal dimensions for a snow block are 40 x 50 cm. A block 15 cm thick will allow some light through

2 Dig a deeper pit at each end. Cold air will sink down here. Lean the snow blocks against one another to form a roof.

Cold air sink

3 Seal off one end with snow blocks. At the other end, cut blocks to make a door with a windbreak. Stuff gaps with snow, but leave holes for ventilation.

Seal most cracks with snow

Camping mat or fir branches

4 Insulate the floor with a camping mat, fir tree branches or a canvas sheet.

MAKE A TARPAULIN-ROOFED SHELTER

To make this shelter you need a tarpaulin and a ski or a stout stick.

1 Lay the tarp on the ground and draw a line around it with your shovel. Remove the tarp. Cut snow blocks and build walls to one metre high, about 0.3 m inside your line.

Snow blocks should be roughly 40 x 50 cm (as before)

3 Add snow blocks to screen the entrance.

Cut entrance with spade or ice knife

Cold air sink

2 Lay the tarp over the walls and anchor it with more snow blocks. Cut an entrance and dig down to make a cold air sink. Raise the ski inside to make a sloping roof that will shed snow. Take care not to pierce the tarp.

Snow blocks shelter the entrance

Entrance prevents drifting snow from entering the shelter

DON'T FORGET

1 Work steadily and rhythmically. Stop to drink water. If you get too hot, remove a layer. Try not to work up a sweat, which will chill you when you stop.

2 Note where you put down tools so you don't lose them under snow. Keep tools inside the finished shelter so you can dig yourself out if necessary.

3 A candle will provide light and warmth in your shelter.

WARNING!

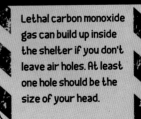

Lethal carbon monoxide gas can build up inside the shelter if you don't leave air holes. At least one hole should be the size of your head.

Making fire

FIRE PROVIDES CRUCIAL HEAT, and melts snow for drinking. It wards off animals from moose to mosquitoes, and allows you to make hot meals and signal your position. But in polar lands, lighting and **maintaining a fire is difficult because fuel is scarce**.

GATHER MATERIALS FOR A FIRE

Tinder, kindling and fuel are all scarce in the polar regions. You need matches, a lighter or fire steel to get your fire going.

Tinder

Grass or moss, dried fungi, thistle-down, bird down, pine resin, an old bird's nest or birch bark will all take a spark if dry.

Bird down

Birch bark

Grass

Moss

Kindling

Dry twigs, bark, pine needles and small scraps of driftwood can be used to stoke the flames. Casiope is a resin-filled heather that burns even when wet.

Pine needles

Twigs

Fuel

Driftwood, pinecones, willow, birch and juniper wood are available on the tundra. Animal fat or dried animal dung burn well.

Pine cones

Juniper wood

WARNING!

Fires are very dangerous. Never light a fire without adult supervision except in an emergency survival situation. Have water standing by to put out the flames if necessary.

TIP

Beat snow off your clothes before standing by the fire. Otherwise the warmth will melt the snow and wet your clothes.

BUILD AND LIGHT A FIRE

1 Site your fire out of the wind. Clear the ground of snow, or build a platform of newly cut branches.

2 Shape the tinder into a ball. Put it in the middle and build a teepee-shape of kindling over it. Crouch to shelter the fire as you light it. Blow gently on a spark to make a flame.

3 Once the kindling is ablaze, add fuel – small twigs at first. You could also build a windbreak of snow blocks or piled snow to screen your fire from the wind.

← To make a spark with a firesteel, sharply draw the striker down the steel.

WOW!

The Inuit traditionally burnt pounded seal blubber in a soapstone container called a koodlik. A scrap of moss or fur was stuck in the blubber to form a wick.

Bow drill

Arctic peoples traditionally used a bow drill to light fires. The string of the bow is wound around a wooden stick, which forms the drill. A bowing action spins the drill in a hollow in a wooden block, producing fine tinder and a spark. This technique takes a lot of skill.

➡ Using and particularly making a bowdrill is an advanced survival technique.

45

Water for life

WATER IS EVERYWHERE IN THE POLAR REGIONS. Unfortunately it is all frozen, so you need to apply heat before you can drink it. Keeping water in liquid form and **preventing it from refreezing is another challenge!**

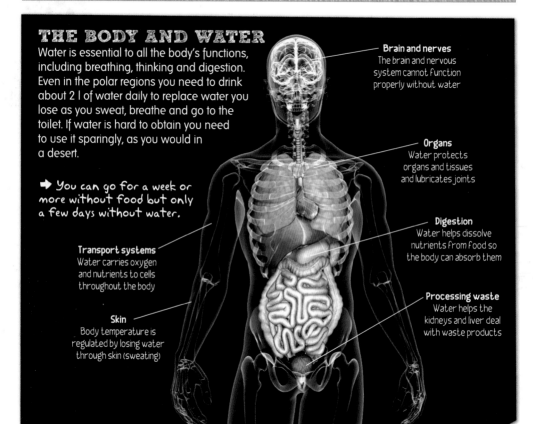

THE BODY AND WATER

Water is essential to all the body's functions, including breathing, thinking and digestion. Even in the polar regions you need to drink about 2 l of water daily to replace water you lose as you sweat, breathe and go to the toilet. If water is hard to obtain you need to use it sparingly, as you would in a desert.

➡ You can go for a week or more without food but only a few days without water.

Transport systems
Water carries oxygen and nutrients to cells throughout the body

Skin
Body temperature is regulated by losing water through skin (sweating)

Brain and nerves
The brain and nervous system cannot function properly without water

Organs
Water protects organs and tissues and lubricates joints

Digestion
Water helps dissolve nutrients from food so the body can absorb them

Processing waste
Water helps the kidneys and liver deal with waste products

Water on the tundra

Finding water on the tundra is easy, but you need to purify it before drinking, by either boiling or using purification tablets. Water collected from fast-flowing streams away from animals is safer than brown-coloured water from still pools. Salt may contaminate water sources near the coast.

TIP

In an emergency, use a sock to filter water. Put fine sand in the toe, then coarse sand, and fine and coarse gravel on top. The water that drips out should be purified.

Water from ice

If there is no water available you will need to heat ice or snow. Choose ice rather than snow – it contains more water, and melts more quickly, thus saving fuel. If you still have some water, heat it in a pan and drop small chunks of ice into it. Keep the water close to boiling, then cool and drink.

➡ Polar survival training involves practising several techniques for melting ice to obtain drinking water.

Bury or anchor the end of the stick to balance it

Container catches drips from melting snow

Water from snow

Arctic peoples obtain water by pushing a large snowball onto a stick, and positioning it near the fire so it drips into a container. You can also place snowballs inside a black plastic bag and leave them to melt in the sunshine.

➡ You could also fill a bag or sock with ice and hang it over a pot. If your bag is plastic, make a small hole in the bottom so water can drip through.

Make a bag from clothing or a mosquito net

End of stick anchored with stones or buried in snow

Fire on platform of sticks

OBTAINING WATER

1 Collect meltwater if you can, for example from dripping icicles.

2 Don't eat ice or snow. You can injure your mouth and warming it will lose body heat, inviting hypothermia.

3 Reduce water loss by removing a layer of clothing when working, so you sweat less.

4 Keep your water bottle near your body to prevent the water freezing. But place it between layers of clothing – not next to your skin.

5 Salty sea ice is no good for drinking. Ice from icebergs contains fresh water. This ice has a bluish tinge.

47

SOLO TO THE NORTH POLE

Naomi Uemura

On 5 March 1978, Japanese climber Naomi Uemura set out to become the first person to reach the North Pole alone on foot.

Progress was painfully slow at first - Uemura only managed 16 km in the first ten days.

DAY 4

A polar bear raided Uemura's camp. It stole his food, ripped open his tent, and sniffed the explorer in his sleeping bag.

DAY 5

The bear returned the next day, but Uemura was ready. He shot it and fed it to his dogs.

DAY 35

Uemura was camped with his dogs on an ice floe when it split apart. He spent a sleepless night stranded on a small chunk of ice.

In the morning he found a narrow ice bridge that led to safely.

At one point on the journey, six dogs fell through the ice. Uemura pulled them out and patted them dry with his mittens.

DAY 57

Reaching the North Pole, Uemura headed south across the high Greenland ice plateau. He completed his epic 6000-km trek in under two months.

GET SETTLED

Advanced camp skills

Making camp

NOW YOU'VE LEARNED THE BASICS OF SURVIVAL, you can move onto more advanced skills, such as building a more permanent shelter. You will need to make a proper camp if you intend to **stay in one place for a while**.

Siting your camp

Choose your campsite carefully, near a source of fuel and water if possible. You need a flattish site where a crag or slope shields you from the wind, but beware steep slopes that could avalanche. Don't camp on an animal trail or near the tracks of bears or wolves. Camp near a stream, but not by still water where mosquitoes breed.

⬇ Water, fuel and shelter are the most important considerations when selecting a campsite.

KEY

1 Rocky outcrop provides shelter

2 Hang food out of reach of animals

3 Be aware – the sound of water could mask other noises, such as an approaching bear

4 Choose an open area to build your signal fire and location aids (see pages 86-87)

5 Site your latrine well away from water

Cave shelter

Caves make great natural shelters, but approach with caution – in winter you may disturb a hibernating bear. Check for tracks outside the cave, but remember that fresh snow can quickly cover paw prints. Light a fire near the rear of an empty cave, not at the entrance, where a fierce blaze could trap you inside.

⬅ Brown bears emerge from hibernation bad-tempered and ravenously hungry. Avoid at all costs.

53

Snug shelters

SNOW IS AN AMAZING MATERIAL that can be moulded to make a strong shelter. An Arctic shelter called a quinzee takes a few hours to make, but is well worth the effort. It will keep you warm when **temperatures dip way below zero**.

BUILD A QUINZEE

1 Mark out a circle for the quinzee, and stamp the snow down. Pile your rucksack, kit and materials such as branches in the middle and cover with a tarpaulin to form a dome.

The dome should be as big as possible while still being strong enough to take the weight of snow

2 Use a shovel or cooking pan to pile snow over the tarp to a depth of about 25 cm, firming between layers. Make a smaller mound on one side to form an entrance. Smooth the surface and leave to harden.

Firm the snow between layers

3 Find at least 20 sticks and cut a notch in each to mark 25 cm. Push the sticks into the dome up to the notch.

Entrance mound should face away from the wind

4 Make an entry hole in the small mound and crawl into the shelter. Remove the kit and branches. Hollow out the inside to the ends of the small sticks.

Don't forget to add ventilation holes

Use excess snow to build a sleeping platform

← Nenet tents are quick to put up and take down, and are loaded onto sledges when on the move.

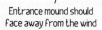

Life in a teepee

In Siberia, Arctic peoples such as the Nenet are caribou-herders. They live a nomadic life, regularly moving their herds to find fresh grazing. They camp in teepee-style tents made of hides slung over wooden poles.

BUILD AN IGLOO

The famous Inuit igloo is used as a hunting shelter. It is made of ice blocks shaped and positioned so they spiral inwards to form a dome shape. Constructing an igloo takes time and considerable skill.

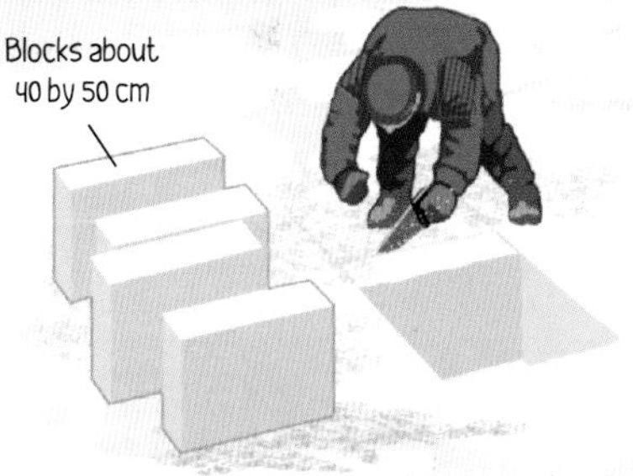

Blocks about 40 by 50 cm

1 Cut hard-packed snow into blocks and smooth the edges.

2 Place the blocks in a circle and shape lower blocks so the next layer spirals upwards.

Upper layers curve inwards

Fit final block from inside

3 Overlap the blocks and shape them to lean inward, creating the dome.

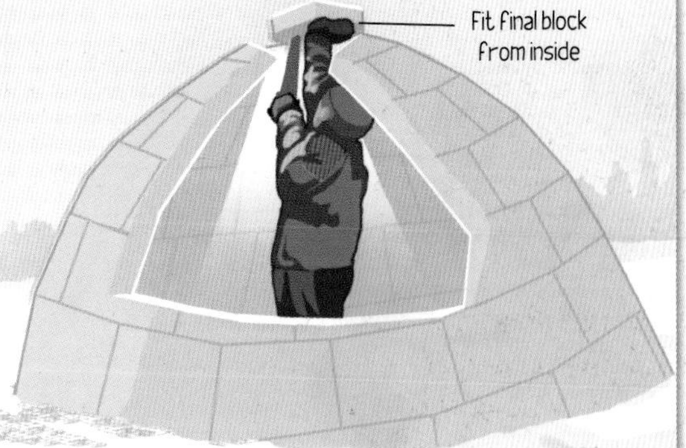

4 Cut a block that is slightly too large for the opening on top. Shape to fit as you move it into position.

Smooth outer surface

5 Shovel loose snow onto the igloo, packing it into all crevices. Smooth the inside by hand and shovel out any extra snow.

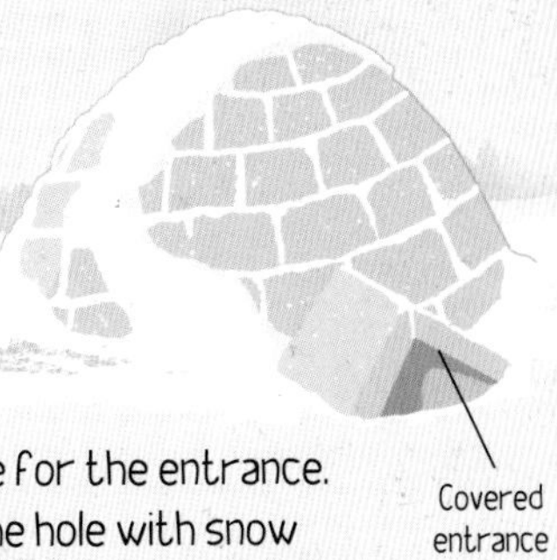

6 Dig a hole for the entrance. Cover the hole with snow blocks. Make ventilation holes.

Covered entrance

THE SKILLS YOU NEED TO SURVIVE in the wild are known as bushcraft. They include building shelters, finding food and making things that make camp life more comfortable. Developing these skills has the advantage of keeping you busy, **which helps you to stay warm**.

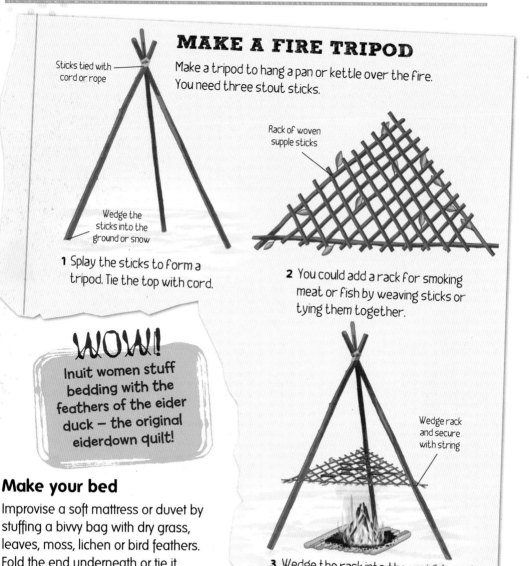

MAKE A FIRE TRIPOD

Make a tripod to hang a pan or kettle over the fire. You need three stout sticks.

Sticks tied with cord or rope

Wedge the sticks into the ground or snow

1 Splay the sticks to form a tripod. Tie the top with cord.

Rack of woven supple sticks

2 You could add a rack for smoking meat or fish by weaving sticks or tying them together.

Wedge rack and secure with string

3 Wedge the rack into the uprights and tie it securely.

WOW!

Inuit women stuff bedding with the feathers of the eider duck – the original eiderdown quilt!

Make your bed

Improvise a soft mattress or duvet by stuffing a bivvy bag with dry grass, leaves, moss, lichen or bird feathers. Fold the end underneath or tie it tightly with string.

A fisherman's knot is useful to join two lengths of rope, cord, wire or string.

1 Take the ends of each cord and place them alonside each other, facing in opposite directions. Loop the end of one cord around the other cord and tie a simple knot as shown.

2 Knot the second cord around the first in the same way.

3 Slide the knots against one another and tighten by pulling on the ends.

➡ This carving of a polar bear comes from the Inuit homeland in Canada, called Nunavut. Many carvings have religious meaning.

Inuit carvings

Carving is an ancient skill in the Arctic. Craftsmen used knives, needles and bow drills to carve tools and decorative objects from driftwood, bones and walrus tusks. The surface was then smoothed and polished using sand and animal hide.

TIP

Wearing supple leather gloves will help to protect your hands from injury when carving.

WARNING!

Take great care when using a knife – any injury can become serious in a remote place. Work with the hand holding the wood behind the blade. Clean your knife after use and put it back in its sheath.

CARVE A WOODEN SPOON

While you're away, you could develop your carving skills by making a spoon from a flattish piece of driftwood. Carving is slow work, but you will produce a useful object that will remind you of your trip.

1 Draw the shape of the spoon onto the wood with a pencil.

2 Gradually pare away the wood to form the bow and narrow handle. Take care – always cut away from your body.

Food from the land

IF FOOD SUPPLIES RUN LOW, you will need to search for wild foods. Unfortunately both plants and animals are scarce in snow-covered regions. Antarctica has almost no plants, and **the only game is found on the coast**.

Game on the tundra

The tundra is rich in game, including hares, rodents called lemmings, and ducks and geese in summer. There are also foxes, weasels, musk oxen, moose and caribou, but beware antlers, horns, teeth and claws!

Caribou A substantial source of meat, but beware hooves and antlers.

Arctic fox Can be eaten, may also lead you to a hidden cache of meat.

Hare Well camouflaged game – has white fur in winter, and turns brown in summer.

Elder duck The fatty flesh of ducks and geese is high in nutrients.

Moose Large, wary and unpredictable. Approach with caution.

Musk ox Defend themselves by forming a circle with horns facing outwards.

EDIBLE PLANTS

Make sure you have absolutely identified plant foods correctly before tasting.

Salmonberries resemble raspberries, but may be red or yellow. They ripen in autumn.

Reindeer moss is a lichen, best boiled before eating.

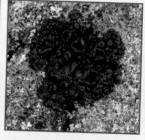

Rock tripe is another type of lichen, best eaten cooked.

The narrow leaves of **Labrador tea** make excellent tea.

TRACKING SKILLS

1. Don't stand in an animal's tracks – follow it at a distance.
2. Move just below a ridge rather than on the skyline, where animals will spot you.
3. Wear camouflaged clothing and move as slowly and quietly as possible.
4. Approach game downwind so it doesn't catch your scent.
5. Use the cover of rocks or slopes to get closer.
6. Freeze if you think you have been spotted, and remain still until the prey loses interest.
7. The best time to hunt is dusk or dawn.

WOW!

Being active and maintaining body heat uses up lots of calories in cold climates. Polar explorers may consume 6000 calories a day – two or three times the normal adult amount.

TRY THIS AT HOME

RECOGNIZE TRACKS

Here you can see the tracks of game animals common in the Arctic. If tracks are partly covered by snow, they may be old.

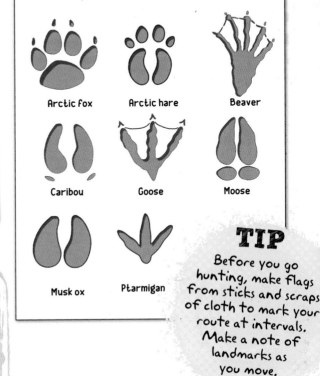

Arctic fox   Arctic hare   Beaver

Caribou   Goose   Moose

Musk ox   Ptarmigan

TIP

Before you go hunting, make flags from sticks and scraps of cloth to mark your route at intervals. Make a note of landmarks as you move.

Bearberries ripen in summer, providing nutrients for bears preparing for hibernation.

Cloudberries resemble amber-coloured blackberries. They ripen in early autumn.

Arctic willow is a low-growing shrub. Its shoots, young roots and inner bark contain vitamin C.

SEALS, WHALES AND FISH are mainstays of the Arctic diet. These creatures can be hunted from the ice or from boats in summer. Fish are less wary than land animals, so fishing offers the best chance of success if you're **in need of a square meal**.

➡ An Inuit hunter crawls toward a seal behind the cover of a hunting blind.

WOW!

The Inuit traditionally hunt seals by waiting by their breathing holes in the ice. When the seal pops up for air, the hunter lunges with his harpoon and quickly hauls the animal out.

Hunting blind

An Inuit hunter may use a blind (camouflaged screen) to sneak up on game. You can make a hunting blind by lashing a square of canvas to a framework of sticks. Make a hole in the middle so you can observe animals. Use white canvas for a snowy landscape, green for a forest.

TIP

Improvise fishing gear by attaching a safety pin, thorn or bent piece of wire to string or fishing line. Bait hooks with animal guts or berries.

⬅ This fine haul of Arctic charr has been caught using a baited line.

Ice fishing

Good fishing can be had through ice that is strong enough to take your weight. Be very careful if you venture out on the ice. Use a large knife to cut a hole in the ice. Drop a weighted, baited line through the hole and settle down. Be prepared to wait!

MAKE A FISHING SIGNAL

A baited line attached to a flag can be left for hours, or overnight if necessary. An upright flag signalling a catch can be spotted from some distance away.

1 Attach the end of your baited fishing line to a stick with a cloth flag tied to the top.

2 Add a crosspiece wider than the hole and drop the weighted and baited line through the hole.

3 The flag will lie flat until a fish takes the bait and pulls it upright – that's how you know you've got a bite!

HUNTING WITH A HARPOON

Improvise a harpoon by lashing a knife to a long, stout stick. Don't risk losing your only knife – only do this if you have a spare.

1 Carve the end flat so the knife fits snugly. Make sure the lashing is very secure or you could lose your knife!

2 Attach rope or cord to the other end so you can retrieve your weapon.

3 Use the harpoon to hunt fish in shallow water. Wait quietly on the bank until a fish comes within range, then lunge to pin it to the bottom.

Cooking fish

Prepare fish by cutting off the head and tail. Slit the belly and remove the guts, which you can use as bait. Bake the fish in foil in the ashes, grill it in a pan, or roast it on a spit. Score the flesh with a knife if you want to smoke it over the fire.

Gills and head should be removed

Slit the underside of the fish from the rear fin to the throat and remove guts

⬆ Fish such as this salmon should be cooked and eaten within hours of being caught.

INTO THE WILD
Christopher McCandless

In April 1992, 24-year-old Christopher McCandless followed his dream to live wild and hitchhiked from Virginia to Alaska.

McCandless came upon an abandoned bus and moved in, planning to survive by gathering plants and hunting game.

Before long McCandless shot a moose, but failed to preserve it properly, so the meat went off.

After three months McCandless tried to leave, but the river he had crossed earlier had become a raging torrent.

He could have used a nearby hand-operated tram to cross the river, but failed to notice it on his map.

McCandless returned to the bus, but he was slowly starving. He left an SOS note outside, but no one saw it.

In September a hunter found McCandless' body in the bus. He weighed just 30 kg. Lack of survival skills and map-reading failure cost him his life.

ATTENTION POSSIBLE VISITORS

S. O. S.

I NEED YOUR HELP. I AM INJURED, NEAR DEATH, AND TOO WEAK TO HIKE OUT OF HERE. I AM ALL ALONE, THIS IS NO JOKE. IN THE NAME OF GOD, PLEASE REMAIN TO SAVE ME. I AM OUT COLLECTING BERRIES CLOSE BY AND SHALL RETURN THIS EVENING. THANK YOU, CHRIS McCANDLESS
AUGUST?

In 1996 writer Jon Krakauer wrote a book called *Into the Wild* about McCandless's experiences. In 2007, the story was made into a movie.

NOTES

GET MOVING

Movement and navigation

Moving on

TRAVEL IN THE POLAR REGIONS is full of danger. Not only is navigation tricky, but you are also likely to encounter perils such as crevasses. And you'll feel the full force of biting cold and blizzards. Before starting on a journey, **consider if it's better to stay put**.

Stay or go?

If you are stranded by an accident such as vehicle breakdown, it's nearly always better to stay where you are. The vehicle will provide shelter and make it easier for rescuers to find you. But if no one knows where you are and rescue is unlikely, you may have to move.

WOW!

British explorer Apsley Cherry-Garrard wrote a book about his trek across the Antarctic ice shelf in the winter of 1911. It was called *The Worst Journey in the World*.

TIP

An imaginary line extending downwards from the tips of a crescent Moon points roughly south in the Northern Hemisphere, and north in the Southern Hemisphere.

ASK YOURSELF	ACTIONS TO TAKE
Does anyone know I am missing or my location?	Wait for help if you will be missed and your location is known.
Do I, or does anyone in my group, have an injury?	Treat injuries. Stay put if injuries are too severe to move casualty.
Can I survive where I am?	Assess location for the basics: water, shelter and food.
Do I know of anywhere better to go?	Move if your location is unknown and/or you will not be missed.

TRY THIS AT HOME **MAKE A HUDSON BAY PACK**

If you don't have a rucksack, you can improvise a Hudson's Bay pack with a one-metre square of waterproof cloth, two small stones and a piece of cord.

1 Lay the cloth on the ground. Place the stones in diagonally opposite corners. Fold the corners over the stones, tying below the fold with each end of the cord.

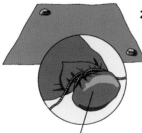

The stones provide 'anchors' at each end of your pack

2 Arrange your possessions in the middle of the cloth and roll them up tightly. Secure the roll by tying extra cord around it.

Sling the pack over your shoulder

Journey preparation

THOROUGH PREPARATION will give you the best chance of surviving a polar journey. Perfect your map-reading skills before you start. Make snowshoes and pack your provisions on an **improvised sledge**.

MAKE SNOWSHOES

Snowshoes spread your weight, allowing you to cross soft snow without sinking in, or 'postholing'.

1 Bend a springy sapling to form a loop and bind the ends tightly with cord.

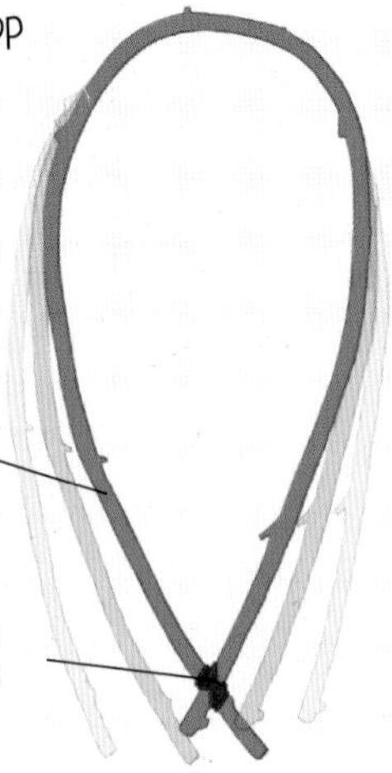

If you can't find a sapling, steaming wood over a fire makes it flexible

Ends tied with string or cord

2 Tie on sticks to form cross-struts, adding more in the central area. Make a second shoe, and rope them onto your feet.

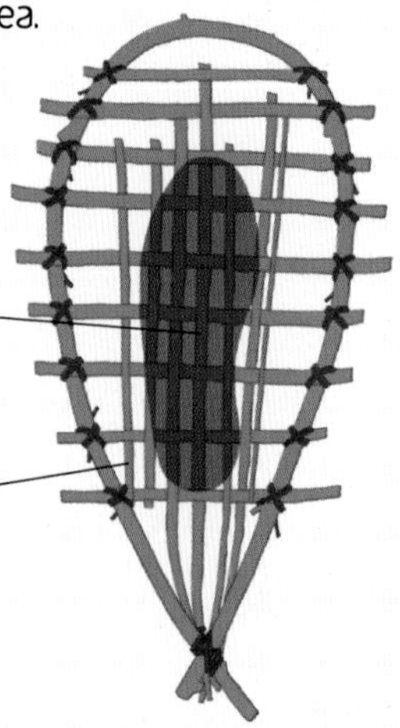

Central area takes your weight

Use as few sticks as possible or your snowshoes will be too heavy

BUILD A SLEDGE

A sledge will make it easier to haul your gear.

1 Find two forked branches and cut off half of each fork to form curved runners.

2 Lash the runners together with sturdy sticks. Add wooden cross-struts to form the top.

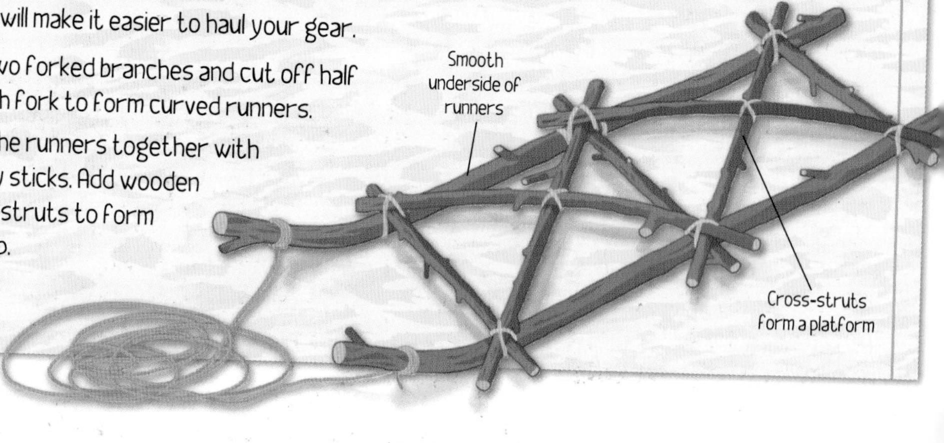

Smooth underside of runners

Cross-struts form a platform

Improve your map-reading skills by learning about scales, grids and contour lines. Practise identifying features such as hills, streams and sheer cliffs on maps of your local area.

Grid lines divide the map into square kilometres. Numbers (and letters) in the margin allow you to pinpoint exact locations (see page 86).

Scales allow you to estimate how long a journey will take. Maps are drawn to different scales. The scale is marked in the margin. On a 1:50,000 map, 2 cm represents one kilometre. On a 1:25,000 map, 4 cm is one kilometre.

Contour lines (brown) link places at the same height above sea level. Tightly spaced contours (for example, in C4) indicate steep slopes. Heights shown in figures will tell you if your route leads up or down.

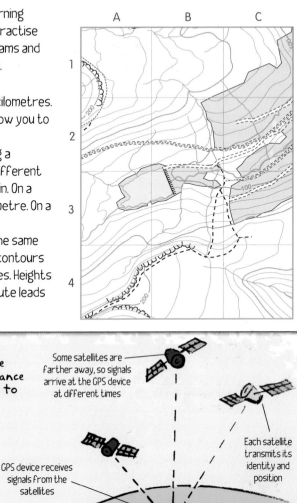

➡ A GPS device locates three or more satellites in space, works out the distance from each and uses this information to pinpoint your position.

Some satellites are farther away, so signals arrive at the GPS device at different times

Each satellite transmits its identity and position

GPS device receives signals from the satellites

Navigation aids

Compasses are unreliable near the Poles, but work on the tundra. If your compass is working, the red needle points north. Use your compass together with a map to work out your direction. If you have a GPS device, make sure you know how to use it. However, this system relies on technology, and is powered by batteries that can go flat in extreme cold.

READY TO GO?

1. Study your map. Check the key to make sure you understand all symbols. Plan each leg of the journey, and don't overestimate the distance you can cover in a day.

2. Don't carry more equipment than you need.

3. Prepare food and water and lash your equipment onto the sledge.

4. Cut one or two stout poles to use as walking sticks if you don't have ski poles.

Finding the way

NAVIGATION IS A HUGE CHALLENGE in the Arctic and Antarctic. If you don't have a reliable compass, you'll have to use the Sun, Moon and stars to get your bearings. There are few landmarks, and **shifting sea ice makes it easy to lose your way**.

Survey the terrain

Before setting out, climb a high point to survey the landscape. Note features such as rivers and ridges, and locate them on your map to check your position. Fix on a distant landmark such as a mountain. Don't use icebergs to get your bearings – they drift with ocean currents and change position all the time.

← Surveying the terrain from a high point will suggest the easiest route to take — here, following the valley.

TRY THIS AT HOME

NAVIGATE BY THE STARS

Learn to recognize some constellations – they could help you to find your way at night.

In the Northern Hemisphere, the bowl of the Plough points towards Polaris (the Pole star) – a bright star that shows due north.

In the Southern Hemisphere, the foot of the Southern Cross points roughly south.

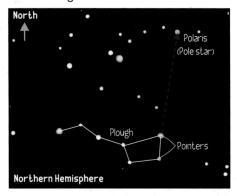

North

Polaris (Pole star)

Plough

Pointers

Northern Hemisphere

South

Southern Cross

Southern Hemisphere

The shadow stick method lets you work out directions without a compass.

1 Push a one-metre stick into the ground or snow. Mark the tip of its shadow with a stick or stone.

2 After 20 minutes, mark the shadow again. A line drawn between the two marks points east-west. In the Northern Hemisphere the first mark is west, the second mark is east. In the Southern Hemisphere it's the other way around.

3 Draw a line at right-angles to show north-south.

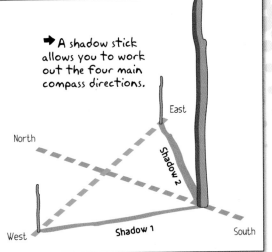

➡ A shadow stick allows you to work out the four main compass directions.

East

North

Shadow 2

West

Shadow 1

South

Stone signposts

The Inuit build stone cairns to mark the way across featureless landscapes. Called *inuksuk*, these cairns sometimes have a human form.

Lighting the way

Looking up into the dark sky, you may observe shimmering 'curtains' of green, red or purple light. These are the famous northern and southern lights, which are caused by solar particles striking Earth's atmosphere high above the Poles.

TIP
Cloud colours can show where land lies. Those over ice and snow have pale undersides because of reflected light. Clouds over ocean or snowless land appear dark underneath.

⬆ A shimmering curtain of light appears over Svalbard in Norway.

⬆ Inuksuk mark traditional routes and are sometimes used to herd caribou.

On the move

"LOOK BEFORE YOU LEAP" should be your motto on a polar journey. With thin ice, seracs and crevasses, it pays to proceed with caution. However, if you move too slowly you **run the risk of getting cold**.

➡ Ski poles or trekking poles keep a firm grip when moving over ice.

Using poles

Ski poles or trekking poles provide extra support when walking, and reduce the risk of slipping and falling. You can also use a pole to test the thickness of ice and the depth of snow or water. Probe the snow before crossing steep slopes you think might avalanche.

Going up

You will need an ice axe and crampons (metal spikes attached to your boots) to tackle mountains or glaciers. Use your axe to chip steps into the ice. Dig the axe in to save yourself from falling. In a group, rope together before crossing steep slopes or glaciers. Descend very steep slopes facing inwards, digging in your toes.

WOW!

When climbing Mount McKinley, Japanese explorer Naomi Uemura lashed long bamboo poles over his shoulders. If he fell into a crevasse, the poles snagged on the rims, allowing him to scramble to safety.

⬆ Two ice axes are needed to scale sheer ice such as frozen waterfalls.

Beware ice ridges

Snow ridges called sastrugi are formed by wind erosion. In places, these ridges may be several metres high – and there may be thousands of them, all facing in the same direction. If you have a sledge you may have to stop, unload, climb the ridge and reload on the far side, which will make progress very slow.

WARNING!

Always wear goggles to protect your eyes from glaring snow and ice. See page 83 for advice on how to treat snow blindness.

⬇ Sastrugi or pressure ridges make the going tough for a team heading for the North Pole.

TIP

Following a river makes navigation easy – as long as it leads in the right direction. Keep to the edge of an ice-covered river, and to the outer banks of bends.

POLAR TRAVEL

1. Wear gaiters when moving through slushy snow.
2. Don't work up a sweat by overexerting yourself. Drink water regularly to avoid dehydration.
3. Leave enough time to make camp before dark. Camp early if the weather takes a turn for the worse.
4. Beware of avalanche in snow-filled valleys and gullies.
5. Distant objects can look close in snowy landscapes. It may take days to reach a mountain peak that looks quite near.

Across ice and water

CROSSING ICE IS ALWAYS PERILOUS. One slip might lead to an icy dip, which could easily prove fatal. In summer, river and sea ice become slushy in daytime temperatures, so **it's safest to travel at night**.

⬇ Wind, waves and sea currents can cause 'leads' of open water to open and close very quickly.

Crossing unstable ice

Jumping between ice floes across 'leads' of open water is extremely dangerous. If you can't avoid doing it, don't go right to the edge. Jump to and from solid ice at least 0.5 m from the edge.

Learn to kayak

Kayaking takes skill and practice. The canoeist uses his or her balance to prevent the narrow boat from tipping over. Practise before your trip – it's best to learn in warm, shallow water!

➡ This experienced kayaker uses balance and his double paddle to steer and stay upright.

⬆ Expert canoers perform an 'eskimo roll' to right an overturned canoe without getting out, but this takes a lot of skill.

Traditional canoes

The Inuit use kayaks to cross open water. These canoes are traditionally made of seal skin stretched over a wooden framework. The covered deck prevents water from swamping the boat, which is powered by a double oar.

SHIPWRECKED IN ANTARCTICA
Ernest Shackleton

In 1914 Irish explorer Ernest Shackleton needed a crew for his expedition to cross Antarctica via the South Pole, and placed an advert in a newspaper.

MEN WANTED

for hazardous journey, small wages, bitter cold, long months of complete darkness, constant danger, safe return doubtful, honour and recognition in the event of success.

In August 1914, the expedition set off in a ship called *Endurance*.

They encountered thick ice in Antarctic waters and in December the ship stuck fast, 160 km from the coast.

The ship remained trapped throughout the Antarctic summer. It was eventually crushed by the ice, and sank in November. The crew were forced to camp on the ice in temperatures of -28°C.

They had to abandon the plan, and wait months until the camp drifted to the edge of the ice.

Shackleton decided the team should make for the Antarctic Peninsula over the ice, hauling three heavy lifeboats. But they managed less than 2 km a day.

Cont. ➡

In April 1916 they launched the lifeboats and made for Elephant Island, 160 km north.

They braved huge waves, icebergs and killer whales.

A week later they reached the island and waded ashore. It was well over a year since they had set foot on land.

Elephant Island had fresh water and food (seals and shellfish), but it was too remote to expect rescue. After a week on land, Shackleton took five men in the strongest lifeboat and made for South Georgia.

After 18 perilous days the small team reached land. But they still had to cross a range of 1200-m peaks to reach the whaling station and summon help for the rest of their crew.

A boat rescued the crew on Elephant Island and in 1916 the expedition arrived back in Britain.

Of the 29 crew not a single man was lost – a tribute to Shackleton's leadership.

NOTES

GET OUT

Health and emergency

HYGIENE AND A BALANCED DIET will help you to stay fit and well on your polar expedition. In an emergency, you will need to call for medical help, but rescue will be slow **in this remote region**.

Keeping clean

Good hygiene helps to prevent stomach bugs and infection. Locate the toilet area away from camp and make sure everyone uses it. Quarry snow for drinking from a different area. If you need the toilet at night or in a blizzard, use a container and empty it when you can!

➡ The crew of a Soviet icebreaker take a snow bath in summer and dry off in the sun.

➡ Citrus fruit and Arctic willow are sources of vitamin C, needed to prevent scurvy.

Scourge of the Arctic

In the 1800s and early 1900s, many explorers and sailors suffered from scurvy – the 'scourge of the Arctic'. This disease causes rotting gums and teeth, internal bleeding and eventually death. In 1932 doctors discovered it was caused by a lack of vitamin C, found in fresh fruit and some Arctic plants and animals.

UV HAZARD

The ozone layer in Earth's atmosphere filters out harmful ultraviolet (UV) rays in sunlight. UV rays can cause skin cancer. The ozone layer is dangerously thin over the polar regions in summer. Put high-factor sun cream on any exposed skin.

➡ In 2007 a satellite sensor captured this image of the ozone hole (blue/purple) at its height over Antarctica. Ozone loss was caused by chemicals called CFCs, which are now banned.

Cold-related illness

MOST HEALTH PROBLEMS on polar expeditions are caused by exposure. Hypothermia and frostbite can set in within minutes in biting winds and subzero temperatures, so you need to **keep a constant watch for early signs**.

HOW TO TREAT FROSTBITE

DO:
1. Get the patient to shelter
2. Supply hot drinks
3. Place a gloved hand over the affected area
4. Place the affected area in a warm place such as the armpit or groin
5. Place the affected area in warm – not hot – water (40°C)
6. Bandage the area and keep it sterile
7. Get hospital treatment for severe frostbite

DON'T:
1. Rub the affected part
2. Burst any blisters
3. Allow a frost-bitten area to refreeze after thawing
4. Walk on frost-bitten toes and feet – unless there is no alternative

TREATING HYPOTHERMIA

Type	Symptoms	Treatment
Mild	Shivering, complaining of cold, slurred speech, cold limbs	Put on extra clothing, give hot drinks
Moderate	Shivering may stop, patient may become confused, incoherent, semi-conscious	Get patient to shelter (e.g. bivvy bag), cover head, replace wet clothing with dry, give hot drinks
Severe	Unconscious, slow breathing, irregular heartbeat	Keep patient warm, place in recovery position, keep airways open, monitor life signs, get patient to hospital

The recovery position

An unconscious casualty on his or her back should be placed in the recovery position. Work from the side.

1. Gently tilt the head back and straighten the limbs.
2. Put the arm nearest you at right-angles to the body.
3. Bring the other arm across the chest and under the cheek.
4. Lift the far leg at the knee and roll the casualty onto his or her side.
5. Bend the upper leg at right-angles to the body.

Arm at right-angle to body

Arm across chest and under cheek

Leg bent at right-angle to body

↑ Check airways are clear before putting a casualty in the recovery position.

Snow blindness

The glare from sunlight reflected off snow and ice can cause temporary blindness, even in cloudy weather. Eyes become irritated and vision becomes misty. Cover the patient's eyes and put him or her in a dark place. The eyes usually recover in time. Guard against snow blindness by wearing goggles or wrap-around sunglasses.

⬇ A snow-blindness victim raises his goggles to reveal inflamed eyes.

TRY THIS AT HOME

MAKE ARCTIC GOGGLES

If you lose your goggles you can make a new pair from a strip of bark, hide or cardboard. Mark the position of the eyes and cut narrow slits using scissors. Use elastic or string to tie the goggles around your head.

Eye slits cut with scissors

String or elastic secures goggles around head

Bark or cardboard

THIS IS TRENCH FOOT

Prevent it!
KEEP FEET DRY AND CLEAN

Trench foot

This condition strikes if your feet are cold and wet for long periods. Blood vessels tighten to restrict the blood flow, increasing risk of frostbite. Dry – don't rub – the feet, and treat as for frostbite. To avoid trench foot, change into dry socks and boots as soon as you reach camp.

⬅ Trench foot was common in the trenches of World Wars I and II. Posters advised soldiers on how to avoid it.

83

In an emergency

'DON'T GET ILL' is the best medical advice on polar expeditions! In practice, this means taking extra care to avoid accidents and infection. In these remote regions, rescue may be impossible. In an emergency, you may have to perform DIY surgery using **whatever instruments are to hand**!

RESCUE FROM A CREVASSE

If one of your team falls into a crevasse, don't go near the edge. Lower a rope, but don't tie it around the casualty's chest, where it could restrict breathing. Instead, make a loop for the victim's foot, and ask him or her to stand in it while you haul them up. Work quickly to prevent hypothermia.

← When the victim gives the go-ahead, haul steadily on the rope to raise him or her from the crevasse.

Victim should hug rope to chest

Many explorers have their appendix removed before a polar expedition to avoid the possibility of a burst appendix, which could be fatal in the wild.

Rescue from water

If a team member falls through the ice, don't go up to the edge. Drive an axe or knife into the ice to anchor yourself, and use a pole or rope to reach them. Treat for hypothermia. If you fall in yourself, use a knife or any sharp object to stab the ice and haul yourself out. Once out, roll in the snow to absorb water. Change into dry clothing and get into shelter.

↑ A European Red Cross team practise rescuing a person who has fallen through the ice.

Gas poisoning

Deadly carbon monoxide gas builds up in poorly ventilated huts and tents. In 1935, US explorer Richard Byrd was poisoned by a leaky stove while living in a remote hut in Antarctica. The rescue party set out when his radio messages became incoherent. But it was a month before they reached him, and he took a long time to recover. Always make sure huts, tents and snow shelters are well ventilated.

TIP
Arctic people traditionally staunch bleeding with spongy moss, and use driftwood or animal bones to splint broken bones.

← Admiral Richard E Byrd was a veteran airman. This photo shows him in the cockpit of a plane, taking measurements.

DIY amputation

In 2000, British explorer Sir Ranulph Fiennes got badly frostbitten fingers while on a solo trip in the Arctic. When he returned home, the condition was so painful he amputated his own fingers using a power saw in his garden shed.

➤ Fiennes has been called 'the greatest living explorer', but self-amputation is NOT recommended.

Attracting rescue

IF ONE OF YOUR GROUP IS BADLY INJURED, you will need to call for help. If your radio or mobile phone isn't working, you'll need another means of signalling. Rescue is most likely to be by plane, so you need clear, effective signals that can be seen from the air. Be patient – **rescue is likely to be slow!**

INTERNATIONAL MORSE CODE

The dots and dashes of Morse Code spell letters and numbers.

The international distress call SOS is short for "Save our Souls".

SOS = ••• ▬ ▬ ▬ •••

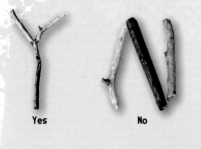

Yes

No

Need assistance

Unable to move/
Medical attention required

Ground to air signals

Bright colours stand out well against the snow. You could spread an orange bivvy bag to mark your location. Branches, rocks or even ash from the fire can be used to spell SOS. Position your signal in the open, where it can be seen from all directions, and make the letters as big as possible.

TRY THIS AT HOME — GIVING GRID REFERENCES

If your radio or mobile is working, be ready to give your grid reference. This six-figure number pinpoints your location. Grid numbers are marked on many maps. Give the east-west distance marked along the bottom first, then the north-south distance up the side. Practise working out the grid reference for the start and halfway-point of a hike.

➡ Rescue flares give off brightly coloured smoke. Make sure the device is pointing upwards.

Using flares

Flares can be seen over a long distance. Read all the instructions carefully beforehand. Hold the flare at arm's length and direct it upright, away from your face. Brace yourself for the kickback when the flare goes off.

Signal fire

Prepare a signal fire and be ready to light it at a moment's notice. Green branches, animal fat or even vehicle tyres produce black smoke that can be seen over long distances.

⬅ A polar expedition team use fire to signal to a ship. Fire signals show up best in darkness.

Select a landing spot

You are most likely to be rescued by a plane with snow skis. Select a level, open place free of rocks or sastrugi for it to land. Mark the landing place with improvised flags. Stand well clear while the plane lands. Helicopter rescue is less likely, but if you are to be winched up by helicopter, allow the winch to touch ground before you grab it, or you'll get an electric shock.

⬆ The smooth surface of a glacier forms a landing strip for a plane fitted with snow skis.

STRANDED IN THE ANTARCTIC
Douglas Mawson

In November 1912 Australian geologist Douglas Mawson led an expedition to the unexplored area of Antarctica directly south of Australia.

On 8 January 1912, the crew reached Cape Denison on Commonwealth Bay, where they built a main base in high winds.

After setting up a second camp on an ice shelf, small teams were sent to survey the surrounding area.

Mawson, Xavier Mertz and Lieutenant Belgrave Ninnis set off east on 10 November 1912.

After five weeks, disaster struck: Ninnis fell into a snow-covered crevasse and was lost, along with the tent, most of the food and the six best dogs.

Mawson and Mertz had to turn back to get a spare tent cover they had left behind, improvising a frame from skis and a theodolite.

Stranded 480 km from base camp with little food, Mawson and Mertz had to kill the remaining dogs for meat and haul their own sledges.

Both men's health began to deteriorate. Around 160 km from base camp Mertz became delirious, then fell unconscious and died.

Experts now believe he died from eating poisonous husky liver.

Mawson dumped most of his few supplies to reduce his load, and set off towards base camp alone.

At one point during the last stage of his journey, Mawson fell into a crevasse. Luckily he was harnessed to his sledge, which became stuck in the ice above him, so he was able to climb out.

Mawson finally reached Commonwealth Bay – only to see his ship sailing off into the distance!

Luckily for Mawson, six men had remained behind at the camp to wait for him. They radioed the ship, but ice prevented its return, and it was another ten months before they were picked up.

NOTES

GLOSSARY

Avalanche When a mass of snow and rock thunders down a mountain.

Blizzard A snowstorm with strong winds and whirling snow.

Bushcraft Survival skills such as hunting, navigating and making things that are useful in the wild.

Calve When glacier ice breaks off at the coast to form an iceberg.

Casualty Someone who is injured.

Conduction When heat, cold or electricity is transferred from one object to another.

Contour lines The lines on a map that join places at the same height above sea level.

Crampons Spikes that climbers attach to their boots to grip the ice.

Crevasse A deep crack in a glacier.

Dehydration Excessive loss of water from the body.

Exposure Lack of protection from the elements.

Floe A chunk of floating ice.

Frostbite When skin freezes because of exposure to the cold.

Grid reference A method of pinpointing location using the numbered grid of a map.

Hypothermia When body temperature drops dangerously low.

Improvise To make something from materials that are to hand.

Insulation Material used to prevent the loss of heat, cold or energy from a surface.

Kayak An Inuit-style canoe.

Kindling Dry twigs that burn well, used to get a fire going.

Lead Gap in sea ice, forming open water.

Morale Good spirits.

Ozone layer Layer in the atmosphere that screens out UV light.

Pack ice Solid ice covering the sea.

Pemmican Pounded meat and fat, once the main food of polar explorers.

Post-holing When you sink into soft, slushy snow, making a deep hole with every step.

Quinzee Traditional snow shelter, made by piling snow around a core.

Sastrugi Ridges in snow or ice, caused by winds blowing in one direction.

Serac An ice pinnacle in a glacier.

Tinder Dry material such as grass, that is used to light fires.

Trailhead Place where the road ends and a hiking trail begins.

Tundra The treeless lowlands of the far north.

Ultraviolet (UV) Rays in sunlight that can cause eye damage and skin cancer.

Whiteout Conditions in a blizzard, when visibility is very low.

ACKNOWLEDGEMENTS

The publishers would like to thank the following sources for the use of their photographs:
t = top, b = bottom, l = left, r = right, c = centre, bg = background

Front cover (clockwise from TL):
f9photos/Shutterstock.com, Frans Lanting/National
Geographic Creative/National Geographic Stock,
nik7ch/Shutterstock.com, Miles Kelly Artwork Bank,
Vitalii Nesterchuk/Shutterstock.com, Miles Kelly
Artwork Bank, Monika Wieland/Shutterstock.com
Back cover (L–R): In Green/Shutterstock.com,
Lipskiy/Shutterstock.com
Alamy 60(t) Louise Murra; 87(t) Ashley Cooper,
(c) RIA Novosti
Corbis 9(br) Alaska Stock; 11(tr) Jacques
Langevin/Sygma, (cl) Bettmann/Corbis; 13(t) George
Steinmetz; 18(t) Wayne Lynch/All Canada Photos;
20(tl) Paul Nicklen/National Geographic Society;
30(br) Staffan Widstrand; 32(t) STAFF/X01095/Reuters;
47(tr) Norbert Wu/Science Faction; 58(br) Keith
Douglas/All Canada Photos; 59(br) Gerald & Buff
Corsi/Visuals Unlimited; 60(b) Staffan Widstrand;
72(t) Henrik Trygg/Johnér Image; 73 Dan
Westergren/National Geographic Society;
74(b) Wolfgang Kaehler; 81(t) Yevgeny Khaldei;
84(b) Oliver Killig/dpa; 85(t) Academy of Natural
Sciences of Philadelphia; 87(b) Stephen
Matera/Aurora Photos
FLPA 53(bl) Ingo Schulz/Imagebroker
Getty Images 16(t); 29(t) Popperfoto; 31(tr) Marilyn
Angel Wynn; 57(c) Marilyn Angel Wynn; 74(c) Danita
Delimont; 85(b)
National Geographic Stock 13(b) George
Steinmetz; 14(t) Gordon Wiltsie; 15(t) Borge Ousland;
17(b) Borge Ousland; 20(b) Paul Nicklen; 25(b) Emory
Kristof; 27(t) Borge Ousland; 39(t) Joe Scherschel; 40(t)
Annie Griffiths Belt; 41(t) Borge Ousland; 58(tr) Norbert
Rosing; 83(t) Borge Ousland
NASA 81(b)
Naturepl.com 45(b) Bryan and Cherry Alexander;
54(b) Bryan and Cherry Alexander
Photoshot 10(br); 15(br); 29(b) Photoshot/TIPS;

58(bcr) Bruce Coleman; 71(bl)
www.rescue-flares.co.uk 26(tl)
Science Photo Library 83(b) US National Archives
Shutterstock.com 11(br) Vladimir Melnik; 12(b) steve
estvanik; 16(b) Volodymyr Goinyk; 17(t) Wild Arctic
Pictures; 18(b) Lorraine Logan; 19(t) Wolfgang Kruck;
(bl) Tyler Olson, (br) LehaKoK; 20(tr) Monika Wieland;
26 (tl–br, from second left) E.G.Pors, Feng Yu,
creativedoxfoto, Daboost, HomeStudio, Petr Salinger,
Vasiliy Ganzha, Bragin Alexey, Lipsky, Sklep
Spozywczy, Stocksnapper, Africa Studio, Keith Bell,
Dja65, Artistic Endeavor, marekuliasz, (tin) Michael
Bann, (inside tin) design56, HomeStudio, Smit, J and S
Photography, Maxim Godkin, Coprid, nui7711,
Ingridsl, terekhov igor; 30(pyramid, t–b) Kesu, Aaron
Amat, Abel Tumik, Aaron Amat, Potapov Alexander,
Imageman, Olga Popova, El Greco, Olga Popova,
Imageman, (bl panel, clockwise from bl) Evgeny
Karandaev, Margie Hurwich, nito, terekhov igor, Lim
Yong Hian, Jiri Hera; 31(first aid kit panel, tl–br)
HamsterMan, Brad Wynnyk, shutswis, Victoria
Brassey, Mazzzur, design56, Alexandr Vlassyuk,
Daleen Loest; 44(tl–br) cosma, Kovalchuk Oleksandr,
ronstik, Nanka (Kucherenko Olena), Olga Popova,
andersphoto, Jiang Hongyan, marekuliasz;
45(cl) Petar Ivanov Ishmiriev; 46 Jeffrey Collingwood;
58(tl) Wild Arctic Pictures, (tc) Sam Chadwick, (cl) Wild
Arctic Pictures, (c) Scarabaeus, (cr) neelsky, (bl) Maslov
Dmitry, (bcl) Taina Sohlman; 59(bl) Sever180,
(bc) Robert HM Voors; 61(br) Edward Westmacott;
70(t) Sander van der Werf; 71(br) Wild Arctic Pictures;
72(b) Vitalii Nesterchuk; 74 zahradales; 81(cl) Albo003;
(dividers) Ari N, Volodymyr Goinyk, Bocman1973,
Roca, Stephen Mcsweeny, Petrenko Andriy,
Volodymyr Goinyk, Uryadnikov Sergey, Alexander
Gorbunov, leospek, Jan Martin Will, Wild Arctic
Pictures

The publishers would like to thank the following artists who have contributed to this book:
Julian Baker, Stuart Jackson-Carter, Nick Spender

All other images from the Miles Kelly Artwork Bank

Every effort has been made to acknowledge the source and copyright holder of each picture.
Miles Kelly Publishing apologises for any unintentional errors or omissions.